Table of Contents

Introduction

The Cricut Maker is considered to be Cricut's flagship model. This is the one that can do just about anything under the sun on just about any material you can fit into the mat guides of your machine. The one drawback of this powerhouse model is the price point. This does make this model more prohibitive, unless you plan to make crafts that you can sell with this model. If this is your intention, you can rest assured that whatever you turn out with this machine will be the best of the best, every single time. If you're selling your crafts, this baby will pay for itself in little to no time at all.

For the avid crafter who likes to show up to the party with the most gorgeous crafts that are leaps and bounds ahead of their peers, this machine might be overkill for the price. Of course, if you are keeping up with the Joneses, this is the model to have.

This model really does have it all and we can prove it. No other Cricut machine has the speed that the Cricut Maker has. The cuts that can be made with the special precision blades that fit only this machine are crisper than anything you could ever hope for from a straight knife or other craft cutter. The blade housings allow you to simply remove the tip from the housing, install the next one, clip it back into place, and keep on rolling through your projects. In addition to this, the machine can detect the material loaded into it, so you won't need to set the type of materials at the beginning of each of your projects. With the other model, a common occurrence is that the project is halfway done before the crafter realizes that the dial is set incorrectly.

With the aid of powerful rotary blades, the machine glides and rolls over any fabrics effortlessly leaving smooth and accurate cut on the material.

There are a lot of models out there, and many great types to choose from.

Cricut has a massive base of users who are enthusiastic to share their projects, tutorials, and tips for care, tricks for usage, and other materials that can be used with their Cricut Makers. The resources for a crafter using a Cricut machine are nearly limitless.

In case you don't have good handwriting, you can also use this machine to that effect. In other words, you can make a Cricut do the job of a printer for you.

What this implies is that any shape or text you desire can be selected from this platform. The specific design you want can then be sent to the machine in order for you to cut it out.

Interestingly, the Explore series of the Cricut machine also makes it possible for direct upload. Hence, you can simply upload the particular design you want and use the machine to cut it out.

The Cricut Design Space allows the user to access any one of the over 50 projects in its library including 25 digital sewing patterns. Not only that, it also allows you to upload an image to create a customized design of your own. The capabilities of the Cricut Maker Machine are just endless: Iron-on decorations on t-shirts, leather, vinyl decors, wood puzzles and sewing projects are some of the DIY or craft projects you can do using the machine.

The Cricut Design Space software can be operated with IOS or Android device having a USB charging.

How Does It Work?

When you see the finished product from a Cricut machine, you will definitely be blown away. The neatness and appealing look of a typical project done with the Cricut machine will take your breath away. However, only a few people understand the process involved in the creation of such amazing designs.

Curious to know how the Cricut machine is able to cut out materials effectively? There are three major steps involved when using the Cricut machine:

Have a Design

If you have a PC, you can access the Cricut Design Space to access the library of designs. If you have a Mac, you can access the same platform to select a huge variety of designs. In case you don't have any of these two but possesses an iPhone or iPad, you can use the Design Space for iOS.

If what you have is an android, you are covered as well. This is because you can take advantage of the Design Space for Android. These are online platforms where you can select any design that best suits your taste.

You can also customize a ready-made design to suit your need. For example, you can resize it or modify the shape. You can also add a text or image as you wish till you have the design just as you want it.

Prepare the Machine

Having selected the design, you intend cutting out with the machine, you are ready for the next step. The machine needs to be prepared by turning it on. Once you switch on the machine, you actually don't need to do anything.

You don't have to press any button unless you are using the machine for the first time. In that case, the machine will give you instructions on what to do. It is that simple.

That is why both beginners and experts can make use of the Cricut machine without issues. Your computer or phone will have to be paired with the machine via Bluetooth for the first time. However, this will not be needed subsequently because the machine will remember the pairing.

Hence, once the machine is switched on, the pairing between the phone and the machine becomes automatic. The implication of this is that once the machine is switched on, the machine is ready. The next step is to send the design to the machine.

Send the Design to the Machine

This is the last stage of the process of cutting with the Cricut machine. Once the machine is powered on, at the top right corner of the screen, you will see the Make It button. This button is a big green button on the Cricut Design Space.

The first thing the software does is to preview the various mats you have. A mat represents a sheet of material; hence, having two different colors in your project implies two mats. There are times that your project can be a combination of a fabric and a paper.

During such occurrences, you will have a mat representing each material utilized for the project. Once you have prepared the machine, you need to decide the dimension with which the machine will do the cutting. If you intend making two cards, the machine has to be instructed to make two project copies.

You will find this option at the top left of the Cricut Design Space. Most of the materials you will be cutting will be cut at 12" × 12" size. This is because this is the standard size that is the most prominent on the Cricut machine.

However, if you prefer a different dimension, you can always alter it. The mirror switch has to be flipped to mirror the design you want in case you want an iron-on design. This has to be done to guarantee that the alteration is reflected by the finished project.

Once you are set to send the design to the Cricut, you will click Continue. This option can be seen at the bottom right corner of the Cricut Design Space. It is easy to continue at this point because the software will prompt you to take you through what ought to be done.

Don't get what up about how to set up different projects of different materials and colors. This is because the instructions you need, will be displayed on the screen and you can easily follow through. Once you follow the instructions presented to you by the machine, you are guaranteed of top-quality cuttings.

The machine will request that you pick the particular material you want to use for the first mat. Simply choose whether it is paper, vinyl, fabric, leather, or any other material. Once you do this, the machine will automatically adjust pressure, speed, and the brush blade as necessary.

Hence, just ensure you do your part of instructing the machine to do your bidding as desired. You can trust the Cricut machine from that point to do all that is needed for a perfect project. After the machine has adjusted itself to cut, you will put the material into the Cricut cutting mat.

At this point, you will then load the machine with the mat. What if I am using different materials for my project? That is also not an issue worth disturbing yourself about.

This is because the software will take you through how to go about loading different materials. Once you are done loading the machine with the mat containing the material, you are good to go. This is because you will be prompted by the machine concerning setting the dial cutting, drawing, or scoring.

The machine will proceed to cut out the mat. The pieces that have been cut out can then be gathered by you and used as desired. This is how the Cricut machine works, and it is basically the same principle for every project.

It is obvious that you don't have to be a genius before you are qualified to use the machine. The instructions are simplified such that anyone who can understand Basic English language can use it. Therefore, if you have been thinking that you might not be able to operate this machine, you are wrong. When you break it down to its most basic operation, the Cricut does two things. It cuts, and it draws. These two functions, however, have over a million uses and can be used on hundreds of materials, making it a truly versatile crafting powerhouse. Breaking it down to these two features seems almost like an injustice to the adaptability and versatility that this machine truly has. If you like to make ornaments during the holiday season, the Cricut can help you make vinyl decals for that. If you like to make ornate greeting cards for every occasion, the Cricut can cut, emboss, score, and engrave accents for any design you can dream up in the Cricut Design Space. If you like making hats and t-shirts for group and family activities, Cricut has a whole range of iron-on materials that can be used for those! Personalize everything you can imagine and more with Cricut products that are meant specifically to help you and crafters all over the world express themselves! There will be no project that can't be made better with a stencil, decal, sticker, or accent created or augmented with the Cricut and its host of customization features!

Chapter 1 Explore Air 2 Machine and Others

Get endless creativity with Cricut Explore Air 2, the fastest Cricut cutting machine ready to create a personal, professionally-oriented DIY project. Cut, write and score amazing designs faster than ever and twice faster than Explore Air, this machine cuts more than 100 materials, from paper and cardboard to rubber and leather. The Air machine is a smart device; select the content you want with different settings on your hand.

It offers wireless editing, writing, and hiding with integrated Bluetooth. This wireless technology allows you to cut complex details with complete accuracy in the creation of stunning stationeries and decorative designs.

In addition to fixing the dot, you can create preferred drop-downs for cards, envelopes, boxes, 3D paper covers, acetate pins, and much more.

It is the easiest and quickest way to turn your creative ideas into reality. You'll be able to change everything in your design from home decor and handmade cards to gifts, fashion, and more. It becomes easier on your computer, iPad, and iPhone, and there are also features that let you design online and offline.

Switching Blades on the Cricut Explore Air 2

Switching blades on the Cricut Explore Air 2 is pretty much tricky. It requires some level of technical know-how and a deep understanding of the blades. Like all machines that use blades for cutting, the blades need to be replaced at a certain interval. Once the blade starts to get blunt, dull or stop cutting, you must know that the Cricut Explore Air 2 is giving you the signs to get replacement blades. Putting the best blades will ensure the best cuts and optimum performance.

If you must switch the blades on your Cricut Explore Air 2, you must be conversant with the types of blades it uses. Each type of blade serves its own purpose, depending on what you want to cut. That is why you must find out which type of blade to switch to next. Note that these blades are sharp, so you have to be extra careful while handling them.

The types of blades the Cricut Explore Air 2 uses include;

Fine-Point Blades: This type of blade is used for cutting paper and vinyl materials. These materials are thin so they can easily be cut by a fine-point blade.

Deep-Point Blades: The deep-point blade is the opposite of the fine-point blade. They are meant to cut thick materials, like card stock and are mostly used in conjunction with fine-point blades for a special or complex project.

Rotary Blades: Rotary Blades or Knife Blades are common blades that are found in Cricut Maker machines. The rotary blade is used to cut fabrics particularly. The knife blade, on the other hand, is used to cut materials that are at least, a millimeter thick.

To switch or change blades in the housing

Locate the cutting assembly on the Cricut machine. The housing assembly is what holds the blades and is like a box that moves along the rod-like shaft.

Loosen the blade housing by pulling open clamp "B".

Press the plunger down on the top and hold.

While holding, the blade will eject itself from the bottom. If it doesn't, gently pull out the blade with your fingers.

Insert the non-sharp end of the new blade into the hole in the bottom. Don't insert the blade with the protective cover. Make sure it's in place. You will know it's in place by the sticking out of the cutting end. It will stick out slightly.

Release the plunger and close the clamp back. By now, the blade must have been snapped into place.

This works on all blades in the housing. Switching from one type of blade to the other is made easy with these steps.

To switch the blades in the Cricut Explore Air 2

Open the clamp.

Add your preferred blade into it and close.

If the blade is not reaching the paper it's meant to cut, it means it is not inserted properly. You have to remove it and try once more.

Cricut Explore One

The Cricut Explore One is Circuits' entrance level spending machine; it's ideal for any individual who needs to begin with a digital die cutting machine yet wouldn't like to spend a huge amount of cash. It accompanies the standard Fine-Point Blade which enables you to cut several materials, and it's perfect with the Deep Point Blade and the Bonded Fabric Blade (sold independently) to enable you to cut considerably more materials.

As its name suggests, the Explore One has a single apparatus holder, so if you need to cut and write in a similar project you should change out the sharp edge for a pen mid-route through the cut. It's extremely simple to change out the accessory or blade, and the Design Space programming will stop the slice and walk you through it when now is the right time, yet if you do a lot of tasks that join cutting, composing, or scoring, it can get tiresome sooner or later.

Moreover, really, the single tools holder is good with the standard estimated edges (Fine-Point, Deep Point, and Bonded Fabric), however to utilize different instruments and extras, you'll have to buy a different connector to fit in the single device holder.

The Explore One doesn't have worked in Bluetooth capacities, so you need to connect the machine to your gadget with the USB link gave. Or then again you can buy a Bluetooth connector independently to enable the machine to cut remotely.

Features

·	Utilize the Cricut Design Space for PC, Mac, iPad or iPhone

·	Transfer your own plans for nothing or pick one from the Cricut Image Library

·	Use text styles introduced from your PC

·	Work on various materials from flimsy paper to thick vinyl

·	With helpful device and extras holder

·	Works remotely by including a remote Bluetooth connector

·	No compelling reason to set with the Smart Set dial or make your very own custom settings

·	Make extends in minutes

Pros

·	Works remotely with Bluetooth connector

·	Transfer your very own pictures and structures for nothing

·	With 50,000+ pictures and text styles from Cricut Image Library

·	No settings required with the Smart Set dial

·	Prints and cuts quick

·	Structure with your very own gadget or PC utilizing Design Space

Cons

·	It expenses to utilize pictures beginning at $0.99

·	Bluetooth connector sold independently

Cricut Expression 1

You can make more customizations for various projects with the Cricut Expression 1. This electronic cutting machine works with the Cricut Craft Room where you can alter plans and improve your output even more. With its six modes and four capacities, you will have the option to make a variety of projects. You can also appreciate quick cutting and plotting speeds which imply that you can make extends quicker, perfect for business use. Expression 1 is additionally portable you can take it any place you should be; at school, at home or at the workplace. It has an LCD screen however touchscreen isn't.

Your buy accompanies a 12" x 12" cutting mat so there is no compelling reason to buy.

The Cricut Expression 1 is portable and woks productively; you can make numerous kinds of activities any way you have to buy cartridges since this one doesn't accompany one.

Features

- Can cut moment 0.25" pictures to 23.5" plans ·

- With ordinary LCD screen ·

- Buy accompanies a 12" x 12" cutting mat

- Compact structure

- Cuts rapidly and productively

Pros

- Totally adaptable to make better plans

- With six modes and four capacities

- Accompanies a 12" x 12" cutting mat

- Works with Cricut Craft Room

- With a convenient plan

Cons

- Issues with the sticky mat

- No cartridges included with buy

- Isn't perfect with different cartridges

- Cricut Easy Press Machine

Cricut Easy Press

Another cutting machine that worth is the Cricut Easy Press. I state that it worth the investment due to the home-accommodating structure and star level execution. It accompanies a major handle, a security base, and an auto-shutoff includes so as keeping your home, workspace, and office very protected. In the event that you request this workhorse, you will get a compact, lightweight and simple to store with a giant, clay-covered warmth plate that gives the definite temperature you need. It is ideal for layered or enormous iron-on projects. It accompanies a reference diagram that will assist you in deciding time and temperature.

Pros

- Ace level execution

- Home-accommodating structure

- Portable and compact

- Reference graph included

- Auto-shutoff highlight

Cons

- Manual warmth temperature and clock settings

- Conflicting weight and little cutting zone

Chapter 2 Projects Explore Air 2 vs. Projects Cricut Maker

Projects You Can Do With Cricut Maker

Felt Roses

MATERIALS NEEDED:

SVG files with 3D flower design

Felt Sheets

Fabric Grip Mat

Glue Gun

STEPS:

First of all, upload your Flower SVG Graphics into the Cricut design space. ("How to import images into Cricut Design Space)

Having placed the image in the project, select it, right-click and click "Ungroup". This allows you to resize each flower independent of the others. Since you are using felt, it is recommended that each of the flowers is at least 6 inches in size.

Create several copies of the flowers, as many as you wish, selecting the colors you want in the Color Sync Panel (by dragging and dropping the images on to the color you would want them to be cut on). Immediately you're through with that, click on "Make it" on the Cricut design space.

Click on "Continue". After your Cricut Maker is connected and registered, under the "materials" options, select "Felt".

If your rotary blade is not in the machine, insert it. On the Fabric Grip Mat, place the first felt sheet (in order of color), then, load them into your Cricut Maker. Press the "cut" button when this is done.

After they are cut, begin to roll the cut flowers one by one. Do this from the outside in. Make sure that you do not roll them too tight. Use the picture as a guide.

Apply Hot Glue on the circle right in the middle and press the felt flowers that you rolled up on the glue. Hold this in place and do not let it go until the glue binds it.

Wait for the glue to dry, and your roses are ready for use.

Custom Coasters

MATERIALS NEEDED:

Free Pattern Templates

Monogram Design (in Design Space)

Cardstock or Printing Paper

Butcher Paper

Lint-free towel

Round Coaster Blanks

LightGrip Mat

EasyPress 2 (6" x 7" recommended)

EasyPress Mat

Infusible Ink Pens

Heat Resistant Tape

Cricut BrightPad (optional) for easier tracing)

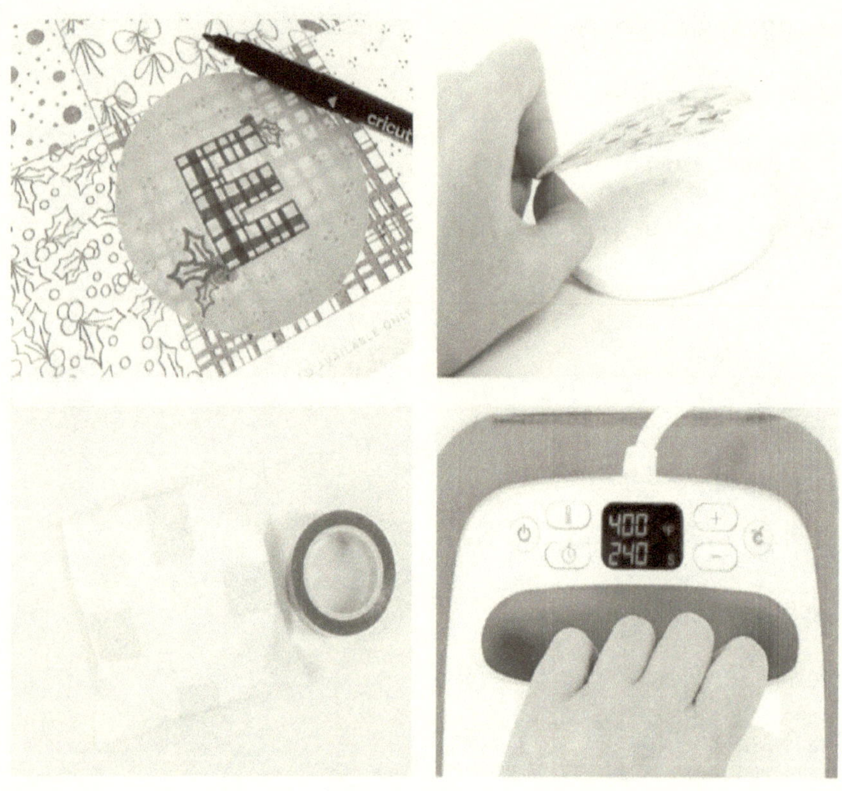

STEPS:

In Cricut Design Space, open the monogram design. You can click "Customize" and choose the designs that you want to cut out or just go ahead and cut out all the letters.

Click on "Make It".

On the page displayed, click on "Mirror Image" to make the image mirrored. This must be done whenever you are using infusible ink. For your material, choose "Cardstock". Then, place your cardstock on the mat and load it into the machine; then press the "Cut" button on the Cricut machine.

After the Cricut machine is done cutting, unload it and remove the done monograms from the mat.

Trace the designs onto the cut-out. If you have a Cricut BrightPad, you can use it to carry out this step much more easily, as it will make the trace lines easier to identify. Tracing should be done using Cricut Infusible Ink Pens.

Use the lint-free towel to wipe the coaster. Ensure that no residue is left behind to prevent any marks being left on the blank.

Make the design centered on the face down coaster.

Get a piece of butcher paper which is about an inch larger on each side of the coaster and place on top of the design.

Tape this butcher paper onto the coaster using heat resistant tape, to hold the design fast.

Set the temperature of your EasyPress to 400 degrees and set the timer to 240 seconds.

Place another butcher paper piece on your EasyPress mat, set the coaster on top of it, face up.

Place another piece of butcher paper on top of these. Place the already preheated EasyPress on top of the coaster, and start the timer.

Lightly hold the EasyPress in place (without moving) or leave it in place right on the coaster – if on a perfectly flat surface – till the timer goes off.

After this is done, gently remove the EasyPress 2 then turn it off.

The coaster will be very hot, so you should leave it to get cool before you touch it. When it is cool, you can peel the design off of it.

Customized Doormat

MATERIALS NEEDED:

Cricut Machine

Scrap cardstock (The color does not matter)

Coir mat (18" x 30")

Outdoor acrylic paint

Vinyl stencil

Transfer tape

Flat round paintbrush

Cutting mat (12" x 24")

STEPS:

Create your design in Cricut Design Space. You can also download an SVG design of your choice and import into Cricut Design Space. Make sure that your design is the right size; resize it to ensure that this is so.

Next, you are to cut the stencil. You do this by clicking "Make it" in Cricut Design Space when you are done with the design. After this, you select

"Cardstock" as the material. Then, you press the "Cut" button on the Cricut machine.

When this is done, remove the stencil from the machine and weed.

Next, on the reverse side of the stencil, apply spray glue. After this, attach the stencil to the doormat, exactly where you want your design to be; then, pick up the letter bits left on the cutting mat and glue them to their places in the stencil on the doormat.

The next step is to mask the parts of the doormat which you do not want to paint on. You can do this using painters' plastic.

Now, it's time to spray-paint your stencil on the doormat. Keeping the paint can about 5 inches away from the doormat, spray up and down, keeping the can pointed straight through the stencil. If it is at an angle, the paint will get under the stencil and ruin your design. Spray the entire stencil 2-3 times to make sure that you do not miss any part and that the paint is even.

You're just about done! Now, remove the masking plastic and the stencil and leave the doormat for about one hour to get dry.

Project You Can Do With Explore Air 2

Cutting Letters and Shapes for Scrapbooking

Shapes are one of the most vital features in Cricut Design Space. They are used for creating some of the best designs. In this tutorial, you will learn how to cut letters or texts, how to add shapes and how to adjust the size, colors and rotate shapes.

To add a shape;

Log into your Design Space.

From the drop-down menu, click "Canvas". You will be taken to the canvas or work area.

Click "Shapes" on the left panel of the canvas.

A window wills pop-up with all the shapes available in Cricut Design Space.

Click to add shape.

We have explained the process of adding a shape. To cut a shape;

Click "Linetype". Linetype lets your machine know whether you plan on cutting, drawing or scoring a shape.

Select "Cut" as Linetype and proceed with cutting the shape.

Cutting Letters

Cutting letters or texts is simple if you know how to do it. To cut letters;

First of all, you need to add the text you want to cut. Click "Add Text" on the left panel of the canvas.

Place text in the area where you want to cut it. Highlight text and click on the slice tool. If you have multiple lines of texts, weld them and create a single layer. Then, use the slice tool.

Move the sliced letters from the circle and delete the ones you don't need.

How to Make Simple Handmade Cards

If you want to test your crafting skills, the Cricut Explore Air 2 has made it possible for you to be creative with designing whatever you want to design on the Design Space. We will be teaching you how to use your Cricut Explore Air 2 to make simple cards.

Log into Design Space with your details. Do this on your Mac/Windows PC.

On the left-hand side of the screen, select "Shapes". Add the square shape.

By default, there is no rectangular shape, so you have to make do with the square shape. However, you can adjust the length and width. You can change the shape by clicking on the padlock icon at the bottom left of the screen. Change the size and click on the padlock icon to relock it.

Click "Score Line" and align.

Create your first line. It's advisable you make it long. Use the "zoom in" option for better seeing if you are having difficulties with sight.

Select the first line you have created and duplicate. It's easier that way than creating another long line. You will see the duplicate option when you right-click on your first line.

Follow the same duplication process and create a third line.

Rotate the third line to the bottom so that it connects the other two parallel lines you earlier created. Remember to zoom in actually to confirm the lines are touching.

Duplicate another line, just like you did the other. Rotate it to the top so that it touches the two vertical parallel lines. You should have created a big rectangular shape.

Highlight your rectangular shape (card). Select "Group" at the upper right corner.

Now, change the "Score" option "cut". You can do this by clicking on the little pen icon.

Your lines will change from dotted to thick straight lines.

Select the "Attach" option at the bottom right-hand side of the screen. The four lines will be attached and will get the card ready to be cut on the mat correctly.

You can adjust the size of the card as you like. At this point, you can add images or texts beautify your card anyhow you want it.

After you are done, select the "Make it" button and then "Continue" to cut your card out.

If you don't know how to create a style on your cards with shapes, follow these simple steps to create one.

Select your choice of shape. Let's choose stars for example. Select the "Shape" option and click on the star.

Add two stars.

Select the first star and click "Flip" and then select "Flip Vertical".

Align both stars to overlap them at the center.

Select "Weld" to make a new shape and add a score line.

Align them at the center and attach them.

Select "Make it button" and then "Continue" to cut your card out.

If you don't know how to add text or write on a card, follow the processes below.

Select your choice of shape. Let's choose hexagon for example. Select the "Shape" option and click on the hexagon shape.

Use your favorite pattern.

Add a scoring line and rotate it.

Click "Add Text". A box will appear on the canvas or work area of your project. Write your desired text. Let's say, you choose to write, "A Star Is Born Strong" and "And Rugged" on the two hexagonal shapes. Choose the fonts and style of writing.

Select the first text and flip vertically or horizontally.

Select the second text and flip vertically. Click, "Flip" and select flip vertically. Doing this will make the text not look upside down?

Attach Select "Make it button" and then "Continue" to cut your card out. Follow the cutting process on the screen to full effect.

Chapter 3 The Business Side of Things and Ideas to Earn

The creativity of your designs and the skill you will develop can allow you to create and start your own business if you wish. For enthusiastic novices, many questions would be faced such as:

1) Where do I start?

Like any start-up business, initial questions need to be addressed to overcome possible difficulties. For example, addressing issues like defining my clientele, the products that might be of interest, where to find them and how to make a profit margin of my sales are important to tackle from the start. In other words, you will need a good and well defined business strategy to start with.

2) Choosing my client

You can target two avenues to sell your products: either by looking at how you can approach the market locally or online. It is advisable to concentrate efforts on one approach to start with as your target is to generate profits as soon as possible. Never forget that your goal is to grow benefit and reinvest it so that your business expands. The quicker you increase your sales, the more likely you will reinvest in new tools or new products, making, in turn, a stronger financial turnover. Understanding your marketing strategy is key to your success.

2.1) Approaching local markets

You can explore selling your products from 'business to business'. In this configuration, the volume of sales is of importance as the larger the production, the lower the production cost per item is. This is the most challenging balance to reach for a new Cricut based business. The advantage of obtaining contractual work means you can negotiate to buy a large quantity from vendors. However, such 'golden' opportunities are hard to find since such contracts are opened to competition. Yet, as a new start-up business, you can present your products specifically tailored for business customers. A custom work approach offers positive aspects as businesses always look for originality and good products. By creating such a relationship, your business is likely to become a point of reference for future other contacts, hence launching many opportunities for upselling. However, it is important to bear in mind that finding such niche is hard as competition is very stiff!

Another approach to consider for selling your products is from 'business to customer'. In this model, though the volume of sales remains important, your objective is to present your products to retail customers willing to buy them. Creativity, imagination will be keys to your success, as well as what type of media and medium you want to work in (e.g. T-shirts, mugs). Equally important is a retail space you will need to choose to offer your items. Experiencing different locations and products is all part of the efforts of a new start-up business. Also, a custom work approach for local customers will present advantages since the startup cost are the lowest of all the different strategies described so far. However, as a new business in the field, starting can be difficult. Word of mouth can be your first step as well as producing good products at an affordable price.

2.2) Selling Online

If you are an adept of higher technical knowledge, then you can generate great benefits by providing either quality custom work, bulk offering or information network. It is advisable to concentrate your efforts on one approach to start with. If you choose, for example, a custom work approach, you increase the chances to find potential customers looking for your products as they turn to a search engine like Google to find what they are looking for. Websites like Amazon Handmade or Etsy provide a good platform to allow selling custom design services. Equally efficient is the launch of your site. This strategy is worth looking at. Selling online presents advantages such as low startup costs and access to the global market with access to millions of potential customers. Furthermore, online custom prices tend to be lower than those on the local market. However, access to the global market means that competition is stiff, pushing products to be competitively priced. Selling online requires certain knowledge in logistics as far as shipping and packing your products are concerned, a cost factor that needs to be taken into consideration in your pricing.

EBay and Amazon have become the largest platforms. On the other hand, if an online retail business approach is more what you may be inclined to do, then this approach will give you the ability to determine the demand for the designs you offer and plan the production accordingly. But selling online means challenging the existing competition!

Finally, if you prefer to sell your products online through information network, then you become an authority in the field, creating the opportunity to generate profit with your Cricut designs. By offering blogs on technical know-how or inspiration work, you become selective on the posts you want to take on.

Starting a new business requires foremost a business strategy, the foundation for your future success. Asking yourself who your potential customers would be, what kind of products you can sell them and how are the first steps of a future startup business.

In terms of making money from the comfort of your home, you easily achieve that with a Cricut machine.   However, you have to bear in mind that there are a number of competitors out there, thus you have to put in extra efforts in order to stand a chance to succeed.

For you to become successful in the Cricut world of crafts, you have to keep the following in mind;

 1. Dare to be different

You have to be yourself, unleash your quirkiness and creativity.

Those that have been in the Cricut crafts world for some time know all about the knockout name tiles. They became a hit and in no time, everyone was producing and selling them.

In the crafting world, that is the norm. Thus, you could be among the earliest people to jump on a trend to ride the wave until the next hot seller surfaces. Mind you, that strategy of selling Cricut crafts can become costly and tiresome if you are not careful.

The basic idea here is to add your flair and personal style, and not to completely re-invent the wheel. For example, let's say you come across two name tiles on Etsy, one looks exactly like the other 200+ on sale on the site, while the second one has a few more tweaks and spins on it. The seller of the second product will possibly charge more and accrue a higher profit because his/her product is unique and stands out from the rest.

When you design your products, don't be afraid to tweak your fonts, because even the simplest of tweaks and creativity can make your product stand out from the rest.

Remember this; if you create a product that looks exactly like others, you are only putting yourself in a 'price war', where no one usually wins.

2. Keep it narrow

A lot of crafters out there believe that creating and selling everything under the sun translates into more patronage, and more money, but that isn't how it works. On the contrary, it might only result in a huge stock of unsold products, more burn out and heavy cost. Rather than producing materials here and there, you should focus on being the best in your area of craftiness, so that when people need specific products in your area, they'll come to you.

It can be very tempting to want to spread your tentacles because it might seem like the more you produce, the more options you'll provide for your clients, but that might be counterproductive.

Take out time to think about your area of strength and focus your energy on making products that you'd be known for. It is better to be known as an expert in a particular product than to be renowned for someone that produces a high number of inferior products.

Thus, you should keep it narrow and grow to become the very best in your area of craft.

3. be consistent

If you intend to become successful, you have to work on your Cricut craft business consistently. Some people work once a week or thereabout because they sell as a hobby; however, if you intend to make in-road in your business, you have to work every day.

 If you have other engagements and can't work every day, then you should create a weekly schedule and stick to it. If you shun your business for weeks and months at a time, then you will not go anywhere with it.

Apart from consistency in work and production, you also have to be consistent with your product quality and pricing. When your customers are convinced about your products, they will easily recommend you to their friends, family, business partners, and many others.

In business, there are ups and downs, thus, you shouldn't reduce your work rate because things are not going as planned. Success doesn't come easy, but one of the surest ways of being and maintaining success is by consistently doing the things you love.

4. Be Tenacious

It is not easy to run a business because it involves a lot of hard work, sweat, and even heartbreaks. Thus, you have to bear in mind that there will be days when you will feel like throwing in the towel. There will be days when nothing go as planned. There will also be days when customers will tick you off. You will feel like a drowning boat because you're working hard but nothing is working out.

However, you have to look at the bigger picture, because the crafting business is not a get rich quick scheme. Remember, quitters never win, so quitting isn't an option. Keep doing the things you love, and keep improving. Successful people never give up. They suffer many setbacks but they don't stop.

Thus, for you to be successful in your craft, you have to be tenacious and resilient. Be willing to maneuver your way through tough times, and do not forget to pick up lessons.

5. Learn everyday

Be willing to learn from people that have been successful in the business. You don't necessarily have to unravel everything by yourself, because whatever it is you are doing, others have already done it in the past.

Whether you intend to learn how to build a successful Facebook group or how to go up the Etsy ranks, remember that people have already done all that in the past, and are giving out tricks and tips they know.

Make it a tradition to learn something new about your business every day because, at the beginning of your business, you will have to do more marketing than crafting.

When you wake up in the morning, browse through the internet, gather materials and read at your spare time, because the more you learn the better your chances of being successful. They say knowledge is power, and for you to become successful as a craftsman/woman, you have to constantly seek new knowledge in the form of tips, tricks, software upgrades, marketing, design ideas, tools, accessories, and many others. All I am saying is that you should learn without ceasing.

Chapter 4 Cartridges

Cricut cartridges are mainly the core of a cricut cutting edge machine, which can be put within the cutter system to form the layout as the consumer wants into a bit of paper.

A wide selection of cartridges can be found on the market all around the earth, although not each one these cartridges operate with all sorts of machines. As an example, the cricut cartridge operates with cricut machines just, and it's the vital element whereby crafters and musicians can create many designs in lovely colors and fashions.

With the fluctuations in printing technologies, a selection of cartridges is introduced recently with more packages to pick from compared to prior ones. The two primary sorts of printer cartridges accessible are: that the ink (utilized from the ink-jet printer) laser cartridges are utilized in laser printers. In the instance of all cricut machines, they still utilize ink-jet printers just.

All roughly cricut ink cartridges:

In the start, cricut ink cartridges were just available in dark, however after some time; a few different colors were released. Afterwards, together with advancement in printing technology, ink cartridges have been created, and attempts have been made to present different font styles, layout and colors for forming contours, too.

The key to success of this cricut system is the usage of different and special kinds of cartridges that empower users to acquire cut and creative in almost any font, layout, color and fashion.

The general types of cricut cartridges are:

* font cartridge: it includes full alphabets, numbers and other symbols together with font styles as well as other font organizing contours. A few of the favorite all-year seasonal and around cartridges comprise little young, jasmine, teardrop, lyrical characters, pumpkin carving for Halloween, thanksgiving holiday, winter wonderland for your Christmas season, etc.,.

Shape cartridge: it includes many different shapes including boxes, tags and bags, animal, sports, newspaper dolls etc..

Licensed cartridge: it enables users to acquire the cut made with favorite figures such as Disney's Mickey Mouse, hello kitty, Pixar toy story, etc...

Classmate cartridge: as its name implies, is specifically created for classroom functions, which includes classroom fonts, shapes and classroom layout, visual analysis program, suggestions and expressions of educators, etc...

Solutions cartridge: it costs less than the remainder. The contours include welding, baseball, soccer, campout, etc...

The broad collection of cricut cartridges, also as mentioned above, provide crafters, particularly young consumers, an opportunity to experiment with their artistic skills without the support of a computer, whereas the cricut ink cartridge which makes it simpler for them to create designs in a variety of shapes and colors.

Selecting the Ideal Cricut for You

Before you buy your very first cricut, it is important to think about all probable alternatives to decide on the very best machine to match your crafting needs.

First, you must stock up to the fundamentals, such as cricut ribbon and picture capsules. These capsules can come in a variety of topics to showcase and commemorate any event, like holidays, holidays or forthcoming events.

You'll also require a huge quantity of colored paper and a pad on which to reduce that contrasts to the dimensions of your system.

If you're an avid scrap booker, then you ought to check into buying a first cricut cutter or even the cricut expression. This system will cut shapes, letters and themes to decorate your videos. You might even decorate bulletin boards, posters, party decorations, greeting cards or invitations of any sort. The cutters can also reduce cloth too. It's encouraged that you starch that the cloth first so as to generate the project as simple as possible to your system to finish. The gap between both is straightforward. The cricut 12 is a brand new, 12" x 24" version of the first cricut. This system makes it easier to make large-scale jobs at a sizable quantity - should you've got the right quantity of paper. Font and picture cartridges may be utilized in the two machines.

Have you heard of this cricut cake? This useful product is designed to cut nearly anything for baked products, such as frosting sheets, gum paste, fondant, cookie dough, tortillas, baking soda, chewing gum and the majority of other soft foods substances. Whatever material you choose to use must be involving 1/16" and also 1/8" thick. Maintain the blade clean constantly so as to make sure the very best cut possible.

Another favorite cricut alternative is your cricut cuttlebug. This system is modest. It merely cuts paper that's 6 inches wide and weighs just 7 lbs. The cuttlebug is mainly useful for cutting and embossing particular crafts. This really is the best method to decorate several greeting cards invitations. Once you include a selection of colored expires, then the cuttlebug is going to be prepared to emboss straight away. These dies will also be harmonious with sizzix, big shot and thin cuts machines that serve a similar function.

Why are you curious and creating your personal t-shirts and cloth designs? Cricut also created the Yudu for all those crafters that love screen-printing and producing their own layouts. The Yudu enables its owners to attach to some laser ink jet printer and generate a layout to screen-print onto virtually anything! Yudus are used for straps, handbags, photograph frames, and shoes - you name it.

Finally, in the event you would like to nourish your newfound cricut obsession, then go right ahead and buy one of those newest cricut gypsys. This useful, hand-held apparatus will keep your ribbon cartridges for simple portable usage. You're able to design from anyplace on the move, in the physician's office, even while on holiday, or merely sitting on your sofa. Anything you plan onto the gypsy is totally transferable to a cricut device for cutting edge. Should you save your layout, it may be linked to some of your cricut apparatus and published at a later moment.

This is a succinct overview of a number of the cutting edge machines cricut presently sells. Because you can see there's a fantastic assortment of machines to get whichever specific kind of craft that you wish to concentrate on. 1 thing is for certain. Whichever machine you select you will have many hours of inspiration and fun producing and creating your own crafting projects.

Although, apparently all of the versions of cricut cutting machines operate in a similar method to some extent using a little bit of variation on precisely the exact same design and characteristics, the cricut design has emerged as a versatile system which has changed the crafting sector by introducing a few new features that improve its functionality.

The cricut machine empowers users to reduce different letters, shapes and phrases in to fine dimensions such as classroom décor, signage, scrapbooks, and much more.

Characteristics Of all Cricut Expression machine:

it's quite simple to work with.

The Cricut Expression Cartridge does not require a computer as it includes Planting School Book and Accent Essentials.

The whole library of present Cricut Cartridge may be utilized.

It empowers users to decrease figures from 1/4 inches from dimension to around thrilling 11-1/2 inches.

It includes LCD display that's easy to see and reveals precisely what's being typed.

Cut landscape and portrait dimensions.

The program supplies a number mode to pick the amount of cuts that the consumer needs of these chosen on the screen.

The auto-fill manner can help to fill pages using as many characters as will fit on the specific page.

By employing this Cricut Expression Cartridge present library that the user may utilize a vast selection of creative attributes in precisely the exact same cut according to choice.

The built in paper saver mode can help you to occupy the smallest amount of space possible in the newspaper.

The line-return work will help to acquire precise spacing by producing line breaks in every single cut.

Fit-to-length along with fit-to-page works readily set how big the duration of a chosen cut on every page.

The other side permits users to acquire a flipped-mode picture cut of their selected shape.

It comes in several distinct languages: French, English, German and Spanish - it's produced in China, also has a 90 day guarantee.

What Makes the Cricut Expression Machine Much Better Than the Rest?

There are certain attributes the cricut cutter features that make it distinct from other Cricut machines:

It's bigger in dimension than many others.

Compared with other machines it may cut much bigger designs around 23-1/2 inches in complete, which empowers the user to make banner layouts, too.

As anticipated, with enhanced attributes, the cutter also comprises a high price tag, too.

Despite all of the gaps together with other existing machines that the fantastic news is it has some resemblance with the old one which makes it increasingly useful. This specific Cricut Machine employs exactly the exact same cartridge as other cutters, so therefore, an individual may update his present Cricut into a new one and utilize his/her assortment of older Cartridges. Even though the Cutter comes with its Cricut Expression Cartridge, undoubtedly, it provides you with additional design choices.

Cricut scrap-booking Machine Review

If you're an avid scrap booker, you need to get one of those machines. They're the greatest garbage booking enthusiast's buddy. They operate simply by loading a cartridge to the machine and picking out literally tens of thousands of possibilities for the decorating ideas.

The phrases and also the border may be an incredible 11 1/2 inches. The cartridges you buy on the Cricut scrap washing machine will provide you the choice of picking from over 250 layouts. And that isn't all. The dimensions of these layouts are from 1 inch to 5 1/2 inches.

How a lot of men and women may create their garbage book as beautiful as possible using this superb machine to provide you with professional results each moment? The broad variety of shapes, letters, layouts, and phrases to grow your scrap book will probably help it become a precious book for several years to come.

This is a fantastic gift idea for anybody who loves crap booking. The newspaper slides and everything you do is pushing a single button. The machine manages the remainder. The portability of this Cricut is yet another notable feature. It weighs just 7 pounds that's excellent for carrying along on a visit from town for a couple of days or into some buddy's home that shares your own hobby.

Another in the household of Cricut products is your Private Electronics Cutter that has exactly the very same dimensions as the standard Cricut machine however, it's the choice of permitting you to cut out of a quarter of an inch up to 11.5 inches. The Personal Electronic Cutter includes a blade which enables cutting edge from eight distinct ways.

The Cuts you are able to make with this particular eight way blade are amongst others these reductions:

Portrait

Fit to page

Auto fill

Center Stage

Flip function

All these features aren't on the normal Cricut cutter. The advancements which were created are great additions like the display screen was improved along with the layout appear to be much skinnier.

Cricut Expressions is a bit larger than the standard Cricut. It wasn't supposed to be portable as the other two; rather it's to remain putting to a desk or inside a meeting area.

Chapter 5 Vinyl

There are different types of vinyl that you can use.

Oracal 651, that I would recommend to use it for PERMANENT works as the strong adhesive might compromise your surface and leave a lot of residue. It is perfect for outdoors works because it is water resistant. But you can generally choose Oracal 651 for your indoor creation that you know you will make a heavy use with, like mugs, plates, bowls. But this might not be working for everyone, so I recommend you first give a try in one mug or two.

Oracal 631 is generally used for wall decals and other internal works and it is appreciated because it can last a little while, but can't stand up to heavy applications. So, it is NOT PERMANENT. However, you can create infinite things with it, like phone cases, interior decorations, stencils, etc…

Heat Transfer Vinyl (More known as HTV)

This is a common and easy to apply method, also for who is starting from scratch. After cutting the piece of vinyl out, you use your iron to apply the vinyl to a fabric surface. It holds up through the washing machine, and looks very professional. You can customize your favorite clothing. There is a variety of brands, but the most often recommended is Scissor EasyWeed. Easy to use, it comes in a variety of styles and colors and it holds up through the washing machine, it looks perfect. It is ideal for: Socks, T-shirts, and Stuffed animals, Canvas tote bags, Costumes, anything with fabric

Printable Vinyl

Printable Vinyl comes both in Heat Transfer and Adhesive types. All you need to have with this particular material is a normal inkjet printer, and the design can be printed out on your vinyl.

Take pieces of vinyl of different colors, cut and put them all on your Cricut Mat, then to make it easier to take a picture of it, I suggest to lay your mat on the floor. Then from your Cricut App, click categories, then Projects in the Cloud, then select the project you are going to cut and click customize, then replace and then Make it.

Next click on Snap Mat and you can place the camera over the floor on your Mat and wait for the box to turn green, hold it for a few seconds and take the picture.

Once the picture popped up, select use, and then select continue. You can start your creation with multiple colors in one mat. You can create images and text and swipe from one color to another.

When you have your image or text over one color and you select it, the selected one will come up with a spin and 3 dots, if you click on the 3 dots you can then select move to another map. Once you have your images and text positioned on each one of your colored mat where you want click continue. It will show that you have vinyl selected and you can go to your Cricut to cut your creation out.

As a novice, your journey to finding the ideal vinyl cutting machine should focus on a gadget with demonstrated execution, notwithstanding long-haul strength. Different variables will help you in your examination of vinyl cutters.

We can sort the vinyl cutters into two primary classes: individual and business models. What do you intend to use your new vinyl cutter for? If you intend to deal with complex structures and signs in large numbers, then you should search for a business model. For a specialist or at-home use, you'll need a customized machine. This model usually comes in a more convenient size, and superbly handles smaller jobs. They are additionally more affordable and easier to use, which makes them perfect for apprentices.

Various models additionally work on different engines, with the two principle choices being the servo and mechanical motor. The advanced servo works easily and gives more exact increases in cutting head and drive motor (improving the general machine precision). Since physical riggings drive the mechanical stepper, it will, in general, be loud during activity. It additionally shows restricted precision when used to cut little pictures. Therefore, I prescribe you to go for the servo motor if possible.

Material compatibility is something most amateurs will overlook when looking for a vinyl shaper. Check what kinds of materials and textures the machine you wish to purchase can cut, aside from vinyl. Search for one that professes to cut plenty of materials. Don't simply accept their claims, however. Check past client reviews on whether it slices through the materials it claims.

Ensure the machine you intend to put resources into accompanies a less intricate activity system and is anything but difficult to use to make accurate cuts. Make sure to peruse different reviews about usability. Check that it is natural to do basic errands like supplanting the cartridges with pens for printing, and stacking papers into the machine. It's likewise fitting to affirm that the machine you need to purchase works with the most widely recognized sorts of papers, such as vinyl, magnet paper, leather, and glue paper.

A few machines even include software that makes your work a lot simpler, and allows individuals to accomplish progressively specialized crafts. They additionally present you with a library of free structures that you can use for snappy activities or as a learner. Different variables that add to the usability of a cutting machine incorporate programmed settings and a remote capacity.

Vinyl cutting machines frequently glitch. That is a reality that most experienced clients will concede to. In that respect, getting a model that accompanies a client guarantee is a significant thought. Other than guaranteeing you the nature of the machine, a guarantee goes about as your safety net. It implies you'll understand what to do if your machine quits working, such as requesting a substitution, or having the proprietor specialists repair the issue.

Notwithstanding how straightforward or propelled a vinyl shaper you're searching for, it must fall inside your financial limit. Similarly, as with the various items out there, these machines will, fluctuate as far as cost goes. The models that come at a greater expense will, in general, be of a higher caliber.

Best Vinyl Cutter Picks

1. USCutter Vinyl Cutter MH 34 in. Bundle

This machine is commonly viewed as one of the most flexible devices ever made. It accompanies vinyl shaper PNC1000 drivers, which enables it to work with VinylMaster Cut just as the various mainstream software, such as Cuts-A-Lot, SignBlaser, Flexi, and SignCut Productivity Pro. This shaper additionally includes two completely flexible squeeze rollers that permit you to cut a wide scope of materials.

The incredibly easy-to-use machine is as extraordinary for specialists as it is for private companies searching for the best value plotter accessible. It can, without much of a stretch, handle all your straightforward tasks. What's more, it doesn't expect you to have any related knowledge before working on it.

With a limit of approximately 31" of cutting width and 8' feet maximum cutting width, you can have confidence that it'll be able to deal with the entirety of your occupations. Extra helpful things included in this bundle include exchange tapes, vinyl rolls, attractive spaces, a squeegee, a blade, and a graph for easy beginnings. Most importantly, it presents you with lifetime phone support, so you'll know what to do when your machine glitches.

Features:

- 34" MH shaper with VinylMaster Cut

- Predominant metal roller double roller framework

- Roland good sharp edge

- Extra things: vinyl rollers move tapes, a squeegee, attractive spaces, a blade

- Lifetime phone support

2. Cricut Explore Air 2 Vinyl Cutter Machine

I suggest anybody searching for an individual vinyl cutter purchase the Cricut Explore Air 2 Machine. It comes uniquely intended to assist you with taking care of all your activities with a definitive speed and exactness. Likely the coolest part about this machine is the way that it permits you to transfer your structures for free. On the other hand, you can browse various (up to 3,000 pre-made) projects, on the off chance that you don't have your pictures or just have a constrained stockpile. You can devise your structures and transfer them using a computer or cell phone.

Something different that makes this machine a most-loved by all specialists is that it permits you to make your designs on more than 100 unique materials, going from the most slender vellum to the thickest leather materials. Since this machine accompanies a two-fold device holder, you'll enjoy up to 2x quicker slicing and composing speed compared to other models.

Features:

- Impeccable individual DIY cutting machine
- Tremendous library of pre-made structures
- Cuts more than 100 materials
- Installed Bluetooth, remote cutting
- German carbide premium cutting edge
- Savvy set dial guarantees simple material settings

3. Cameo with Electronic Vinyl Cutting Machine Starter Kit Bundle

To be completely forthright, it wasn't justified, despite any potential benefits. All the present cutters are the same. They use similar software, have a similar size, and work at a similar precision and speed.

So what makes the Cameo II stand apart from the remainder of the cutting tools? The ability to begin your printing venture straight out of the box is a blissful euphoria for some DIY creators. It's extremely simple to learn and utilize. If you have a tad of structuring information and add some creativity to it, you're ready.

This Cameo accompanies a starter unit, vouchers for downloading structures on Silhouette's website, and one month's worth of free membership to their download store. It's a plug and-play machine, much the same as your printer. The vinyl shaper can slice material up to 10' wide and 12" in length. Supplant the sharp edge with a pen, and this machine will outline your structure as opposed to cutting. It includes a vinyl trimmer edge, 51 selective

Cuttable plans, a dark cutting edge, a cutting mat, premium exchange paper, and more. It's too great of a deal to pass up.

Features:

- The Cameo II starter unit comes prepared with all that you have to get moving
- Simple to learn, regardless of whether you have had structuring information
- Good software that supports both Mac and Windows
- Vinyl cutting sharp edges are replaceable

4. Brother CM350 ScanNCut 2 Home and Hobby Vinyl Cutter Machine

The Brother CM350 ScanNCut 2 Home and Hobby Cutting Machine also rank among the top spots with other great vinyl cutters available today. The main thing that caused me to notice this model is its built-in 300 DPI scanner, which permits you to make your cuts effectively. As it were, you can examine simply anything, including cherished family photographs, carefully assembled drawings, home layouts, and so forth, and go through them to accompany exceptionally detailed cut shapes and frameworks that fit your particular project.

We likewise appreciated the reality that this machine comes structured as a stand-alone model. In any case, it additionally gives you the option of connecting it remotely to your computer. Other incredible highlights right now include a super-huge LCD touchscreen display, 600+ included structures, and the capacity to plan SVG information documents.

Features:

- 4.85" LCD touchscreen display

- 300 DPI scanner

- PC compatibility; wireless network display

- 600+ structures and 7 integrated fonts

- ScanNCutCanvas cloud

- Web-based application that allows the client to manage PDFs

Chapter 6 Buying the Best Cricut Machine

The Cricut machine isn't the least expensive. You can likewise however at shopping center deals if web-based purchasing alarms you somewhat. Keep in mind, it about looking and being tolerant simultaneously. Upbeat scrapbook making!

Your budget and how you intend to use the machine are big factors; however, you'll find most Cricut machines are around the same price except for the Cuttlebug Machine.

This is a small, portable hand-crank machine that has a maximum cutting width of six inches. It only works with dies and embossing folders; however, it's perfect for those who are looking for a machine they can use for scrapbooking and card making.

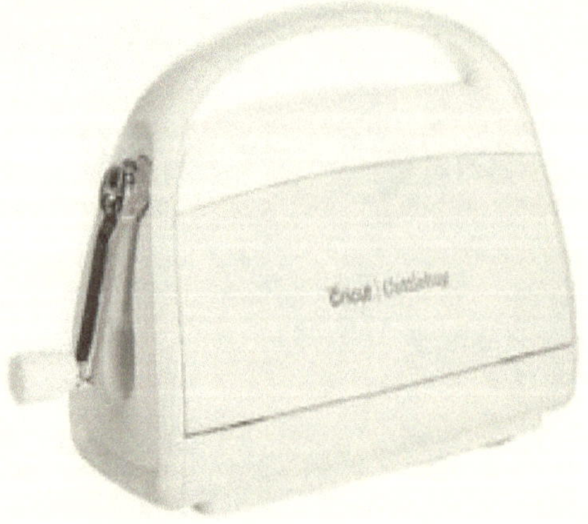

The hand-crank machine has been a staple in the Cricut family, and you can usually find a new one for under $100. A used hand-crank can be far less money. If it's in good condition and that's what you want, you can sometimes find them for as low as $25 at garage sales and garage sale sites.

Cricut maker

This year, a new model was released called The Cricut Maker™. This has all the bells and whistles to do most anything. It has the capability of cutting more materials than any previous models and the company boasts its fast, precise cutting.

The Cricut Maker is Cricut's flagship model. This is the one that can do just about anything under the sun on just about any material you can fit into the mat guides of your machine. The one drawback of this powerhouse model is the price point. This does make this model more prohibitive, unless you plan to make crafts that you can sell with this model. If this is your intention, you can rest assured that whatever you turn out with this machine will be the best of the best, every single time. If you're selling your crafts, this baby will pay for itself in little to no time at all.

That in mind, the Cricut Maker, costs $399.99. That is a large sum of money for someone who doesn't have it and even to someone who does have it. Although there's a lot you can do with $399.99, there are just as many things you can do with the Cricut Maker. My advice would be to save until you can afford it or put it on your wishlist in the meantime and subtly hint to your loved ones that you'll absolutely love to have one of these bad boys. Hopefully, someone will catch on and not balk at the massive amount of dollars that it will eat up.

The Cricut Maker can be used with your images, which is a plus for those who prefer to use their own or don't want to buy a subscription or pay for individual images. It allows you to personalize your items and make your statement. You can make personalized cards, signs, and anything your heart desires. The ability to personalize your items with multiple lines and fonts broadens your horizon. If you make products to sell, you can offer personalization.

Cricut Cake

If you do manage to find either one of these machines, you can expect the price to amount to nothing less than $142.99 for the Cricut Cake Mini and $199.99 for the Cricut Cake Personal Electronic Cutter.

All in all, I think that if you can get your hands on the Cricut Cake that will be incredible. It's not without its faults, but for a cake decorator and simple crafter, the Cricut Cake is perfect. The materials above can be cut just as good as with any other machine if you switch out the blade and use the right pressure, speed, and mat. You might struggle with slicing items that the machine was not designed to cut, though, so keep that in mind. There will be a limit when it comes to the variety of materials that you will be able to craft with, but it does work just fine with the things listed above.

The Cricut Cake is perfect for cutting unique details for any cake that you are decorating, especially for lettering and making silhouettes that are difficult to free hand. The fondant cutouts can also be used to dress up cupcakes. Whatever the occasion may be, the Cricut Cake machine can cut your decorative fondant or gum paste perfectly.

Cricut Explore

With all the capabilities of the Cricut Explore One and more, the Cricut Explore Air model comes equipped with Bluetooth capability, has a built-in storage cup to keep your tools in one place while you're working, so they won't roll away or get lost in the shuffle.

This model does have two on-board accessory clamps, which allow for simultaneous marking and cutting or scoring. These clamps are marked with an A and a B so you can be sure your tools are going in the right places, every time you load them in.

This model is equipped to handle the same 100 materials as the Cricut Explore One, and operates at the same speed, so the price difference reflects those differences and the similarities! This is a great value for the powerhouse that you're getting.

At the time of writing this, the cost for the Cricut Explore Air is $249.99

Cricut Explore One

In terms of what is currently available from Cricut, this is the most basic machine they offer. This machine boasts being able to cut 100 of the most popular materials that are currently available to use with your Cricut machine, as well as being perfectly user friendly.

The Cricut Explore One is the no-frills beginner model of Cricut craft plotters and operates at a lower speed than the other models available. Unlike the others available in the current product line, the Cricut Explore One has only one accessory clamp inside, so cutting or scoring, and drawing cannot be done simultaneously. They can, however, be done in rapid succession, one right after the other.

While this is a great tool for a wide range of crafts on 100 different materials, and which can get you well on your way to designing breathtaking crafts that are always a cut above others, the cost is not as high as you might imagine. If you intend to use your craft plotter mainly for those special occasions where something handcrafted would be perfect, then this a great machine to have on hand. The cost for the Cricut Explore One is $179.99

Cricut Explore Air 2

This model cuts materials at twice the speed of the previous two models, has Bluetooth capability, and has the two on-board accessory clamps.

The storage cup on the top of the machine features a secondary, shallower cut to store your replacement blade housings when they're not in use, so that if you happen to be swapping between several different tips for a project, they're all readily available to you throughout your project. Both cups have a soft silicone bottom, so you won't have to worry about the blades on your machine becoming dull or scratched!

For someone who finds themselves using their Cricut with any regularity, this is the best machine for the job. You will be able to do your crafts twice as fast, and you will get a satisfactory result every time, even at that speed!

At the time of writing, the Cricut Explore Air 2 is priced the same as the

Cricut Explore One, at $249.99. If you're looking to jump on this, now is the time to get the best deal.

Whatever you can afford. There is no wrong way you can go. It all depends on what you want to do with the machine and how much money you are willing to spend.

Choose wisely

It takes structures that you make or transfer (like those you get free from us) into their Design Space programming and removes them.

Would you be able to transfer my pictures to use with Cricut?

Indeed! You can transfer your pictures, or any of our free SVG and me cut records that are as of now arranged to be perfect with Cricut Design Space.

What various materials would i be able to cut with Cricut?

Everybody will in general consider Cricut machines as cutting paper or vinyl. Yet, the fact of the matter is there are a LOT more things that a Cricut can cut. The Cricut Explore Air 2 can cut more than 60 sorts of materials!

Will it be simple for me to figure out how to utilize Cricut Design Space to make my custom ventures?

That's right, and I'm here to help! Look at our Cricut instructional exercises page here, which is a great spot for learners to begin! We include new recordings every week and even give accommodating free assets and agendas, so ensure you return frequently.

With the current line of available models, the Cricut Design Space allows you to be an innovative as you can be with the design process, so none of your creative flow is eaten up by operations that should be taken care of by your machine.

Chapter 7 How to Set Up the Cricut Machine

I am going to help you set up your machine and we will make it as easy as possible so that this will not only go smoothly but so that you can enjoy your machine without frustrating yourself. There are two different ways to do this and it depends on what technology you are working with. If you are working with a Mac or a Windows you need to set it up one way, and if you are running on an Android or an iOS you will have to do it another way. Many people think that this process is difficult but it's quite simple and takes ten steps or less which is great right? How easy is that?

However, in case the door does not open automatically, put mild pressure on it to completely open the door. Then, place the keyboard overlay on the top of the keypad of the machine. At this point, the cartridge of the machine should be inserted into the cartridge slot.

The cartridge slot can be found in the front of the Cricut machine. However, you must ensure the title on the cartridge agrees with the one on the keypad overlay.

The first way we will show you how to how to set up your machine if you're working with an Android or an iOS. This can be a very frustrating thing when you are trying to set things up and this is something that we want to avoid. So let's get started so you can get your machine ready.

Plug Your Machine In And Turn The Power On.

You will need to pair your device (either Android or iOS) with your machine. You are going to need to utilize your Bluetooth to do this.

Download the Design Space App. You will need to install it into your machine as well.

Hit the Button That Says Menu.

Select the button that says machine setup and app overview. Now, you are going to select the button that says new machine setup.

The next step is pretty simple because the only thing that you will have to do is follow what your screen says. There are going to be on-screen promptings that will help you to complete the setup. Just be sure that you are following them accurately and if you can't go quickly that's fine. Go at the pace that you're comfortable with so that you can make sure that you understand what it is they are wanting from you. Going slower will help eliminate mistakes but if you do make mistakes don't feel bad. This happens to people every day and it's easily fixable.

You will know that you've done everything right and correctly when it is telling you that it's time to make your first project. Once this happens, you know that your setup is complete. Once you've done this it's time to get crafting!

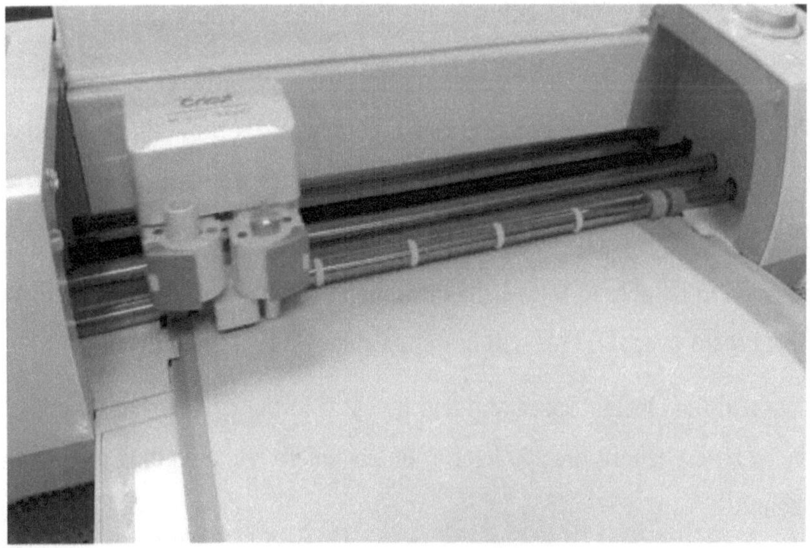

An additional tip for you is that your machine is already automatically registered during the setup. If you don't complete the setup when you connect your machine you need to reconnect it. Because the machine has to be registered this is something that you can't miss.

If you're working with a Windows or a Mac you will need to follow these following instructions to make your machine work. This setup is easy as well and offers one less step than the instructions above and since Macs are considered to be newer this will be a little bit different than the instructions above.

Plugin your machine. Don't turn your machine on or try to without plugging it in first.

Power the Machine On

Connect your machine to your computer. You are going to do this in two different fashions. This is an excellent option because you can choose which option is the best for you. You can either do this by using the USB cord or do it this way or you can connect your machine by pairing it by using Bluetooth. Either of these ways will work well it's just whatever you would like it to be.

Go to the website design.cricut.com/setup in your browser because this is going to be how you are going to finish your set up. From this step, you will be able to complete your setup by making sure you are overseeing the instructions.

You need to be able to follow the on-screen prompts and instructions to sign in and create your ID. This will be your Cricut ID for the future.

Download the Design Space app and install it to the device. This is going to have so much benefit for you later as this is where you are going to gain a lot of benefits.

Don't forget that you will need to plugin when it prompts you to do so.

You will be able to see that you did everything right and correctly when it wants you to make your first project. Once you reach this step your machine is ready to go, and you can make the practice project so that you can get used to your machine and how it works without wasting materials.

The very tip above about the registration applies here too and if you have a problem setting up on any of the systems you can come back to this site so that you can be able to set it up without trouble or issues. Having the website tell you what you need to do and having the prompts is a great helper to new users or older users of the machine as they offer help pages as well. With simple steps and back up help however starting your machine is easy as can be which is a great benefit to the user. These models are made to be as user-friendly as possible to eliminate the issues that other companies have when their items are being set up.

By now you should have the app installed on your phone or the software already running on your laptop or desktop computer. If you have not yet, you better do so now because things are about to get a lot more serious, and it would help if you have Cricut Design Space in front of you to experiment what we will be discussing.

What's more, you should do this, especially if you are a beginner. Perhaps intermediaries or somewhat experienced users can afford not to have the app or software in front of them right now.

Downloading/Installing

Do you actually know where to get the Cricut Design Space? Well, if you are on a desktop or Personal Computer, navigate to https://design.cricut.com. If you are using an iOS device such as an iPhone or iPad, find your way to your

App Store and input "Cricut Design Space" on the search space.

If your smartphone runs on Android OS, enter the Play Store and use the same search term. Remember that downloading or installing this is entirely free of charge. Also, bear in mind that you will need a Cricut ID to sign in. This you can also get for free, even if you do not have a Cricut. Simply follow the prompts provided.

Once you have entered your email and gotten your ID, you will at once be taken into the primary domain of the Cricut Design Space, the place where all of the magic happens. Quick tip: bookmark this page to your web toolbar so you can find it easily whenever you want to.

The Canvas you will be shown after - similar to a painter's whiteboard - is the big space where all your designs and progress will reflect - this space has a full grid by default to allow you see everything about a single work without having to pinch-zoom and un-pinch. Nevertheless, you can choose the appearance and measurements of the grid.

Smart Guides And Shortcuts

So you want to try out your first design, and you happen to be stuck while trying to position something on your canvas correctly? In Cricut Design Space, this could happen because the Smart Guides are just too smart for their own good. Want to know what the guides are about?

Quick one: Smart Guides are a feature of the Android and iOS app version of the product. They are designed to help you when you want to position things in relation to other things. But that could not turn out or position the way you want it to. If you want to turn this off on the app version, go to Settings - at the bottom areas of the toolbar - and toggle the Smart Guides off.

Meanwhile, there's something about the desktop version of Cricut Design

Space that makes it somewhat cool - it has some keyboard shortcuts that will definitely come in handy. If you want to see them at any point of use, tap on the question mark key on your keyboard - Shift +. Shortcuts that will prove useful to you include the show hide menu, toggle grid, and select all options.

Other shortcuts also allow you to save and "save project as", undo - this is something you will be thankful for - redo, cut, copy, and paste. What's more, bring forward, send back, bring to front, send to back, and of course, delete.

If you are the kind of technophile who's more used to the keyboard than clicking on a mouse, you will find these shortcuts super useful.

How to Position Items on the Cricut canvas

Not to discourage anyone, but it can take you several months of using the Cricut Design Space almost every day before you will find this useful, and probably a little more time before you can get used to it.

Well, this little nugget actually informs you on how to move and rotate your items on the mat preview. This is done in order to position your cuts and pen write when you want or feel the need to.

You know when you are working on a project and just want to flip things up fast? This feature lets you do so quickly and effortlessly - well, almost (insert smirk emoticon here).

This comes significantly handy when you want to use up scraps and just spread them all over your canvas. If you are working on an address envelope, for instance, you can use this tool so that your letters reflect on the "write" side on the envelope. You may also want to reposition - do so by tapping and dragging an item on your canvas to a new location. Simple enough, isn't it?

On the desktop version, move the objects to another mat and conceal them altogether - just click on the three dots, they are not hard to find since they are virtually in your face. So, now you know how to best position those items to make your design all the more easier.

Chapter 8 Creative Ideas to Do on Your Cricut

Now that you know what a Cricut machine is and how to set it up, it is now time to delve into the best part of the Cricut—making your designs! We will look at the materials that you can use, what can be cut, and what crafts can be made. In all honest—the options are endless as crafters are continually coming up with new ideas and new craft using the Cricut, so each time, you'll find something new.

Cricut Paper Crafts

What do you need? You need some standard weight paper, or you can also use cardstock. Cricut has both these options which you can purchase. You can use this, or you can use any paper you like. Here is a selection of ideas that you can kick start your Cricut paper crafts. Just click on the links of the specific craft to get more details:

- Creating a 3D Paper Bouquet

Cricut is an excellent tool to make beautiful, one-of-a-kind paper bouquets simply because they have plenty of flower patterns you can choose from. You can make these paper bouquets using paper of any kind and in any color. Using different hues from the same color would be ideal because it gives you depth and texture.

- No-Sew Paper Garland

See all these fantastic paper garlands during weddings and events? How do people do this many garlands? Well, they probably used the Cricut. No-sew paper garlands brighten up any space and you can use different kinds of shapes to create your garlands. Once you cut it out using your Cricut, all you need to do is string thread through these cut-outs and hang them up. That's how it's done!

- Personalized Napkin Rings

If you do not have a design in mind to make your napkin rings, head over to the Cricut Design Space, type in 'napkin rings,' and you'll find a host of designs that you can tweak and use to your liking. Making your napkin rings with initials or even images of your own to make your event personalized.

- How to Make 3D Flowers

Cricut flowers, while beautiful, can be a little tedious and tough to assemble. Thankfully, this handy, step-by-step guide provided by Hey Let's Make Stuff is useful for crafters looking to add some paper floral arrangements to their dining table centerpiece, a mantel, or decoration on a wedding vase.

- Lampshade

This craft requires you to work on an existing lampshade and upgrade it. All you need is a lampshade that has seen better days and think about you want to redecorate it. You can paint the lampshade with fabric paint and then print out different motifs, such as butterflies to paste on the lampshade, to give it a beautiful 3D effect.

- Paper Marigolds

Take your decoration game to the next level with Cricut. Put on a great show for the Day of the Dead by taking out your Cricut and making beautiful yellow and orange marigold paper flowers. With the Cricut, you can make these paper flowers as realistic as can be and as big and bold as you want it to be. Making paper flowers large, and as many as possible, will be quickly done with the Cricut. The hardest part is assembling them according to its sizes.

- Notebook Revamp with the Cricut

With some black vinyl and notebooks that you have lying around, you can amp up your notebooks to the next level. How? Use the Cricut on its vinyl settings, place your black vinyl on the grip mat, and get to work. By the end of the day, you can have a bunch of fashionable, black-letter notebooks worthy of being in a bookstore.

- Paper Swag

This paper swag can be any motifs you like, but leaf motifs are among the favorites. Find a leaf collage on the Cricut Design Space, cut the motifs out, and use a scoring tool to score a line straight to the middle of the leaf to fold on the lines. You can use floral tape and wire to secure leaves, and use ribbons or any other adornments to make the swag beautiful.

- Paper Succulent Centerpieces

Don't like gardening but still like the look of succulents? The Happy Scraps has a fantastic tutorial on how you can create a paper succulent centerpiece. Cricut even has succulent colored cardstock, which you can use to create this look precisely the way Happy Scraps has done. Make these flowers and place them the way a succulent garden would look—in a beautiful container.

- Pop-Up Cards

If you love making cards and giving them to your near and dear or even selling them on your Etsy store, then investing in a Cricut is the way to go. You can make pop-up cards of any kind and any cardstock. All you need is a little bit of creativity. Like this pop-up rainbow card, it is so versatile you can make it any motifs such as shades of red hearts for Valentine's Day, snowflakes for Christmas greeting cards, four-leaf clover shapes for St. Patrick's Day, or even book shaped motifs where you can add in your favorite short quotes.

- Luminaries

Do you ever look at luminaries and think 'How beautiful they are' and wonder how those intricate paper carvings were done? Luminaries are great for the holidays or for table centerpieces at a restaurant, and they are among the popular decorations for weddings as well, to light up the aisle, as table decorations, and so on. In this tutorial by Jennifer Maker, she uses layers of beautifully cut panels to provide contrast and texture. You need vellum to complete your luminaries, and also because this is paper—do not use candles, but LED candles would be a better and safer option.

- Cricut Vinyl Crafts

One of the most common projects plenty crafters choose to work on is with vinyl with the Cricut. Cricut offers an amazing variety of vinyl to choose from, and they are all in excellent quality. You can get the standard vinyl, more premium ones, glitter vinyls that are the crowd favorite, printable vinyls, dry erase ones, and chalkboard vinyls. Here is a selection of things you can do with them:

- Pantry Labels

This craft idea makes for an fantastic beginner's craft. Labels are one of the most natural things to make with the Cricut and the most straightforward. All you need for this is Vinyl, transfer tape, label designs that you can get from the Cricut Design App, and your machine.

- Vinyl Board

You can use any board to create a vinyl of words or images to update your board. Using chalkboard is one of the favorites as it creates a beautiful decor for the home. You can cut out words from your vinyl and stick it on to your board. It can say 'Welcome Home,' or 'Grocery List,' or even a motivational quote.

- DIY Drink Coasters

Coasters are another kind of beginner's craft to do with your Cricut. You can personalize it any way you want, such as using fonts, images, colors, or glitter vinyl—the options are endless. You need a standard grip mat to work with, the essential cricut tools, the type of vinyl you want to use, and some transfer tape. Of course, your choice of coasters is also essential for this project, so don't forget this. Clear varnish is also needed to finish the project.

- Playroom Accent Wall

This accent wall for your child's playroom makes a colorful statement to brighten up your kid's day. The most tedious part of this project would be measuring and painting the wall. After that, the fun part begins with the Cricut machine to do fun decorations. The primary Cricut Essential Tool set is a must to have in vinyl projects as it makes taking out intricate cuts out smoothly and efficiently.

- Memory Game

This is a fun kid's craft project that uses a vibrant lime vinyl. In this craft, you make tiles featuring animal images. Cricut released its Cricut Vinyl Brights which includes 12" x 12" sheets of vinyl in vibrant colors from Grape, Sunshine, Caribbean, Lime, Flamingo, and Azure. These colors are fun which is perfect for summer crafts.

- Chalkboard Robot Town

If you want to color up and decorate your children's room walls, using Cricut Vinyl for wall decals makes decorating these walls easy. All you need to do is design or find symbols that you like, resize it to the size you want to fit your walls, cut it, weed it, and stick it. For projects involving murals, it is always best to measure your space and create a design on your Design Space App, placing the motifs or symbols or images to where you envision it on the wall, on your canvas in the app. Once you are happy with what you have, connect it to the Cricut, cut it out, weed it out, and then start sticking.

- Personalized Sports Gear

Yes, you can your sports gear scream your name! Have you joined a group workout or sports clubs and brought your gear along only to find it's gone missing because someone mistook your stuff for theirs? Well, if you have ever found yourself in a situation like this, it's best to get your gear emblazoned with your name on it, so nobody mistakenly takes it again. This is a perfect idea for your luggage too. Use the vinyl Cricut settings to create your name with an image of your choice—anything that stands out against the color of the object you want to personalize so it is visible and it can be spotted from a distance.

- Holographic Phone Case

If you are one of those people who love changing your phone cases, the Cricut makes it possible for you to have every season or whenever you feel a change coming your way—except with half the cost and exactly the way you want it to look. Holographic cases have become quite popular, and Cricut crafters have a bunch of tutorials and SVG files that you can use, like this one from Laura's Crafty Life. To do this project, you would need a clear phone case of course that suits your phone size, as well as holographic vinyl. Explore the designs you like to use and use your Cricut to make this happen.

- Decorated Vinyl Flower Pots

If you love keeping plants and have a few indoor plants all around your home, time to give them an upgrade by adding some fun motifs to your pots. Some people add intricate designs, some add gold bands to give it some extra class, some put on labels, and some just put on fun motifs. You can use any vinyl that fits your creative ideas and use your Cricut to get this idea to reality.

Cricut Iron-On Crafts

Another must-do and popular craft among the Cricut fraternity is the iron-on. Iron-ons are among the most popular after paper or even vinyl crafts simply because you can use it on everything from wood ornaments to T-Shirts, jeans, tote bags, and onesies. You can even make your holiday gifts with the Cricut Iron-On crafts for your family and friends.

Chapter 9 Getting to Know Design Space

Design Space gives crafters a canvas upon which to design their crafting projects. It is simple to use and easy to learn the basics. Like any new system or software, there will be a learning curve but the more you use the system the easier it will get. Let's takes a look at the Design Space screen layout, the canvas, and introduces you to some terminology commonly used with Cricut machines and Design Space.

Getting Started With Design Space

On January 29, 2020, Cricut ended support for the Design Space web experience that could be accessed from www.design.cricut.com

You can still access this software, for now, for all those who are still running on a Windows 7 machine. This end of software support coincided with the end of Microsoft support for Windows 7. For those who have Windows 7, you may find that the system is sluggish and there will be no further updates on the platform.

The new version of Design Space is referred to as Design Space for Desktop and can be run straight from the desktop on a MAC or Windows machine. This gives the software the ability to run off-line. This gives crafters a lot more freedom as they don't have to rely on an internet connection to work on their Cricut cutting machine projects.

You do, however, still need an internet connection for the initial download of the software. You will also need internet access to ensure your software is updated with the latest patches, fixes, and updates from Cricut. With the new desktop Design Space application, you can run it as you would any other desktop application you may use.

What Is Design Space?

Design Space is the design software that comes with every new Cricut cutting machine. There is a downloadable app for both desktop and mobile devices which can be used both offline and online.

Most of the Cricut cutting machine models that came out in the last four to five years have Bluetooth connection capability. With the ability to connect wirelessly, the Cricut cutting machines can be used with iOS and Android devices. They are also compatible with MAC and Windows systems through both Bluetooth as well as USB connectivity.

Why Use Design Space?

The first few models of the Cricut cutting machines came with their own screens, keyboards, and graphic cartridges. They did not need a design package to create various crafts. Although they were remarkable craft machines for their time, they also had limited crafting and cutting abilities.

The latest model of Cricut machines have more advanced capabilities with a streamlined design that allows for more cutting space and a wider range of cutting materials. They no longer have a built-in screen or keyboard. Models like the Cricut Maker and Cricut Joy no longer come with a cartridge slot either. They rely entirely on the Design Space image, project, and font libraries to function.

Design Space gives the crafter more control over their crafting projects. The software comes loaded with a library containing thousands of images. The software also includes hundreds of already created projects that can be customized to suit the crafter's needs. Design Space gives the user control over their projects and as such, they are not limited to what is on a cartridge.

The Design Space image, fonts, templates, and project libraries are frequently added to.

Design Space is easy to learn and use. It is free to download and comes with free images, templates, fonts, and shapes. Design Space does require the user to create an ID to log in. This login ID allows users to save projects as well as images, fonts, or ready-made projects they may have purchased. Most of the machines come with a free trial membership to Cricut Access which gives its members access to free Cricut Access images, fonts, and projects. You do not have to be a Cricut Access member to buy any fonts, images, or projects. The beautiful thing about Design Space is that you can buy an individual image, font, or project as or when you need them.

New Features in Design Space

Design Space has launched the new Design Space for Desktop. As this is new, there are still a few bugs and updates that Design Space will roll out in the near future, which is why it's called Desktop Beta.

What Is Different in Desktop Beta?

Design Space Desktop can now be run directly from the Desktop and does not require the user to log in from the Design Space website. This makes Design Space available in offline mode without an internet connection.

The Desktop Design Space application gives the user the ability to save their projects both on their PC and keep them in the cloud. This makes working with your favorite projects easy both offline and online.

Images can now be downloaded for offline use as can projects and fonts.

Downloading Design Space Desktop Beta

Downloading Design Space Desktop Beta requires an active internet connection.

Minimum System Requirements for Design Space

Design Space is compatible with Windows, MAC, iOS, and Android operating systems. In order to run the software on these systems, devices must meet the following minimum system requirements:

Windows Operating Systems

- Microsoft Windows version 8 or higher

- The device must have Bluetooth or USB support

- The CPU should be either Intel Dual-Core or AMD processor of equivalent specifications

- The device must have at least 4GB RAM

- The device must have at least 2GB free disk space

- The screen display should be able to support a resolution of at least 1024px x 768px

MAC Operating Systems

- MAC OS 10.12 or higher

- The device must have Bluetooth or USB support

- The CPU should be at least 1.83 GHz

- The device must have at least 4GB RAM

- The device must have at least 2GB free disk space

- The screen display should be able to support a resolution of at least 1024px x 768px

iOS

- iOS 11 or higher

- iPhones from the iPhone 5s and newer models

- iPad mini 2 and newer models

- iPad Air and newer models

- iPad Pro 12.9" and new models

- iPad 5th generation

- iPod touch 6th generation

Android

- Android 6.0 or higher

- Mobile devices

- Tablets

- Chromebooks are not compatible

Downloading and Installing Design Space

To access the Design Space software for a computer or mobile device, you will need an active internet connection.

Downloading and Installing Design Space for Windows

The download is run from https://design-beta2.cricut.com/#/launcher.

Choose Download to start the Design Space for Desktop download.

When the system is downloading, the screen will prompt "Downloading Design Space for Windows". This can take a few minutes depending on the connection and your device.

Once the download is complete, go to the Downloads folder on the PC and double click on the file — Cricut Design Space Install v4.2.4.exe (the version number may differ depending on the updated version).

There may be a pop-up window asking for permission to trust the application — select to trust the application or it will not install.

Follow any on-screen prompts, selecting the default settings until the software starts to install.

During the installation, there will be a pop-up box with an installation progress bar to show how far the installation has progressed.

Once the installation is complete you will be asked to "Sign in with your Cricut ID".

First-time users of the software will need to create a Cricut ID by clicking on the button below the sign-in sheet on the screen.

The Cricut desktop icon automatically gets added to the Windows desktop or can be found under the 'All Programs' taskbar where you find your installed programs.

To access Cricut Design Space, click on either the desktop icon or the program under the All Programs taskbar.

Downloading and Installing Design Space for MAC

The download is run from https://design-beta2.cricut.com/#/launcher.

Choose the option to Download.

When the system is downloading, the screen will prompt "Downloading Design Space® for MAC". This can take a few minutes depending on the connection and your device.

Once the download is complete, go to the Downloads folder on the MAC and double click on the file — Cricut Design Space Install v4.1.6 (the version number may differ depending on the updated version).

When the Cricut icon appears, drag it into the applications folder and the installation will begin.

Once the installation is complete, you can drag the application icon to the dock to create a shortcut or access the program from the application folder.

The first time you use Cricut on a MAC you may get a warning "Cricut Design Space is an app downloaded from the internet. Are you sure you want to open it?" — Click on the Open button to continue to Design Space.

On the first Design Space screen that appears, you will be asked to "Sign in with your Cricut ID".

First-time users of the software will need to create a Cricut ID by clicking on the button below the sign-in sheet on the screen.

To access Cricut Design Space, click on either the desktop icon or the program under the Applications folder.

Downloading and Installing Design Space for iOS

On an iOS compatible device, you will need to go to the App Store.

In the Search option, find the Cricut Design Space app.

To download and install the app, select Get. You may have to verify the download depending on your iTunes set up.

When the app has finished downloading and installing, you will be directed to the "New Machine Setup" page. If you do not wish to go through the setup right away, you can either go to the app overview screen or click on the X in the top right-hand corner to exit.

You can access the Cricut app by clicking on the application icon on your iOS mobile device.

Downloading and Installing Design Space for Android

On an Android device, you will have to access the Google Play Store to get the Design Space app.

In the Search box, find the Cricut Design Space app.

To download and install the app, select Install and the application will start to download.

When the app has finished downloading and installing, you will be directed to the "New Machine Setup" page. If you do not wish to go through the setup right away, you can either go to the app overview screen or click on the X in the top right-hand corner to exit.

You can access the Cricut app by clicking on the application icon on your Android mobile device.

Design Space Tips

Design Space will automatically pick up your operating system when you first download it.

Design Space remembers your login details so you will not have to enter them every time you log in. You can opt not to use this option should you prefer to log in every time.

You should save your work on a regular basis when working in the application as it does not have an auto-save feature.

Chapter 10 Maintenance of Cricut Maker

Every Cricut Maker needs to be cleaned and taken care of in order to keep it working for as long as possible.

Here, you'll learn about the maintenance required for Cricut Maker, and what you can do to keep your machine working efficiently.

Cleaning and Care

Cleaning your machine is very important, and you should do it regularly to keep everything in tip-top shape.

If you don't take care of your machine, that's just money down the drain. But what can you do to care for your machine?

Well, I do suggest initially that you make sure to run maintenance on it as much as you can and keep it clean.

There are a few other tips and tricks that can help prolong the machine's life. For starters, keep liquids and food away from the machine – never drink or eat while you use your Cricut machine.

Set up your machine in a location that's free of dust and try to keep it away from excessive coolness or heat, so don't just throw it in the attic or an exceptionally cold basement.

If you're transporting your machine to use it at a different location, never leave it in the car.

Excessive heat will melt the machine's plastic components, so be careful.

Finally, make sure the machine is stored away from sunlight. Keep it out of places in the home where sunlight hits it directly.

For example, if you have an office that is very bright and the sun warms the machine for an extended period of time, you'll want to move it so that it doesn't get damaged.

Be gentle with your machine. Remember, it is a machine, so you'll want to make sure that you do take some time and try to keep it beautiful and in order.

Don't be rough with it, and when working with the machine parts, don't be too rough with them, either.

Caring for your machine isn't just about making sure that the parts don't get dirty, but you should also make sure that you keep everything in good working order.

Cleaning the Machine Itself

In general, the exterior is pretty easy to clean – you just need a damp cloth. Use a soft cloth to wipe it off, and keep in mind those chemical cleaners with benzene, acetone, or carbon tetrachloride should never be used on your Cricut machine.

Any cleaner that is scratchy, as well, should be avoided at all costs. Make sure that you never put any machine components in water.

This should be obvious, but often, people may use a piece of a damp cloth, thinking that it'll be fine when in reality, it isn't.

You should consider getting some non-alcoholic wipes for cleaning your machine.

Always disconnect the power before cleaning, as you would with any machine.

The Cricut machine can then be lightly wiped down. Some people also use a glass cleaner sprayed on a cloth but do be careful to make sure no residue builds up.

If you notice there is some dust there, you can typically get away with a cloth that's soft and clean.

Sometimes, grease can build up – you may notice this on the cartridge bar if you use cartridges a lot.

Use a swab of cotton or a soft cloth to remove it.

Greasing the Machine

If you need to grease your machine, first make sure that it's turned off and the smart carriage is moved to the left.

Use a tissue to wipe this down, and then move it to the right, repeating the process again.

From there, move the carriage to the center and open up a lubrication package.

Put a small amount onto a Q-tip.

Apply a thin coating, greasing everything evenly, and also clean any buildup that may have occurred.

This is usually the issue if you hear grinding noise when cleaning the machine itself.

There are a few other famous places that you should make sure to clean, besides the outside and the carriage.

Any places where blades are should be cleaned; you can just move the housing unit of the blade to clean it.

You should also check the drawing area, to make sure there isn't any excessive ink there.

Never use spray cleaner directly on the machine, for obvious reasons.

The bar holding the housing shouldn't be wiped down, but if you do notice an excessive grease, please take the time to make sure that it's cleaned up.

Remember to never touch the gear chain near the back of this unit, either, and never clean with the machine on, for your own safety.

When caring for a Cricut machine, try to do this more frequently if you're using the machine a lot, or twice yearly.

If you notice strange noises coming from the machine, do get a grease packet. You can always contact Cricut and they'll help you figure out the issue, if there is one, with your machine.

Cricut machines are great, but you need to take care in making sure that you keep everything in proper order.

Cutting Blade

Your blades will tend to dull over time, but this is usually a prolonged process.

The best way to prevent it is to have different blades to cut different materials.

Having a different blade for each material is a perfect idea. You can get

fine-point ones which are good for smaller items; deep-cut, which is great for leather and other fabrics; bonded fabric, so great for fabric pieces; a rotary blade for those heavy fabrics; and finally, a knife blade, which is good for those really thick items.

In order to maintain your blades, you should clean the housing area for every blade after each use, since they get gunky fast.

Squirting compressed air into the area is a beautiful way to get the dust out of there.

As for the blades, remember foil? Use a little bit of that over the edges of the blade to help clean and polish them up.

To polish them, you should put them on the cutting mat and from there, cut small designs on it.

It actually does help with sharpening them, and it doesn't require you to remove them altogether.

You can do this with every single blade, too!

To change the blades in their housings, just open the clamps, pull up, and remove the housing within the machine.

Put a new blade in, and then close it.

That's all it takes. Storing them is also pretty simple.

There is a drop-down doorway at the front area of the machine. It's made for storing the blades within their housings.

Put your loose blades in there first, and then utilize the magnet to keep them in place.

The best part about this storage is that your blades are always with the Cricut, even if you take the machine somewhere else.

There is also a blade organizer that you can use, too, made out of chipboard with some holders attached. This is also a wonderful means to store all of your items.

Organizing your Cricut blades is very important, and understanding the best places to keep them is, of course, essential.

Cutting Mat

Your cutting mats need to be cleaned because if you don't clean them frequently, they will attract dirt and lose adhesiveness.

That means you'll have to spend more money on mats, which isn't ideal.

There are different ways to clean them, and we'll go over a few of the different means to clean your mats so you can use them for longer.

Cleaning the Mat Itself

First, if your mat is completely filthy, you need to clean it. Of course, you'll also want to do this for just general maintenance, too. Once it's been cleaned, you'll notice it's sticky again.

Typically, washing it down with either a magic eraser or a kitchen scrubber can do it.

Sometimes, if it's really dirty, you might want to get some rubbing alcohol onto a wipe.

If you notice a chunk of the debris left behind, however, is fabric oriented, hen get some lint rollers or even just stick some scotch tape on there and pull it off.

This can eliminate the issue.

But what about the really tough grime? Well, get some Goo Gone cleaner. Put a little bit on the troublesome spots and wipe it around, and then let the goo stick on there.

From there, get an old card or something to get it off, and then wash the mat. Once it's dry, check to see if it's sticky. If it is, then great – you don't need to do anything more.

But what if you notice that it's still not sticky? Well, why not restick the cutting mat itself!

Resticking the Mat

To do this, you need to make sure that you tape the edges, so you don't get adhesive near the edges, and mess with the rollers of the machine. Once that's there, use either spray adhesive or glue stick, and then let it dry.

If you notice that it's still not sticky enough when you're finished applying the first coat, apply a second coat.

There are great adhesives out there, such as simple spray adhesive, easy tack, quilt basting, bonding, and also repositionable e glue.

All of these are fairly effective, and if you notice that the mat is actually sticking pretty well, then you're in luck.

However, always make sure that you let this fully dry.

If you don't let the adhesive dry and you start using the mat again, you will run into the problem of the material being stuck to it.

Once it's dried, try it out with some test material.

If you find it too sticky at this point, but either your hands or a shirt on there to help reduce the tackiness.

Caring for Machines and Mats

Here are a couple of other tips to use with your cutting mats.

The first, use different mats. You may notice that you can get more out of one type of mat than another kind, which is something many people don't realize.

Often, if you notice that you get a lot more out of the firmer grip mats, buy more of those.

Finally, halve your mats.

You can save immensely by making sure that they're cut in half. This does work, and it helps pretty well. You can expect anywhere from about 25 to 40 different cuts before you'll need to replace the mat, but cleaning after about half of that can definitely help with improving the quality of your cuts.

The life of the mat, of course, does vary based on the settings and what materials you cut. When you can't get it to stick, try cleaning and resticking it, but if you notice that it's still not doing the job, you're going to need to get a replacement.

Taking care of your Cricut machine will get you more use out of it, so make sure you perform regular maintenance on all your machine's components so it can be used for years.